TRUE
Covenant

Colin Urquhart

Kingdom Faith Resources Ltd.
Roffey Place, Old Crawley Road,
HORSHAM West Sussex, RH12 4RU
Tel: 01293 851543 Fax: 01293 854610
E-mail: resources@kingdomfaith.com
www.kingdomfaith.com

First published in Great Britain in Oct 2002 by Kingdom Faith

Kingdom Faith Trust is a registered charity (no.278746)

ISBN ????

Acknowledgements

Words cannot express my thankfulness to God for drawing me into covenant with Him, and for all the wonderful blessings He has poured into my life as a result. It has been a great joy to share truths about His covenant promises and faithfulness in this book.

My thanks to Mary who has learned to interpret my handwriting (I was invented before computers!), and to David and Cliss for all they have done in the presentation of this book. Whatever I do I am encouraged by the loving support of all who pray for me, and especially my wife Caroline, my family and Paula, my assistant, and all with whom I am in covenant relationship at Kingdom Faith.

Colin Urquhart

CONTENTS

1

WHAT IS A COVENANT?

Jesus came to inaugurate a new covenant. At many celebrations of the Lord's Supper or Holy Communion, His words are quoted: *"This is my blood of the new covenant, which is poured out for many for the forgiveness of sins." (Matthew 26: 28). Or, "This cup is the new covenant in my blood." (1 Corinthians 11: 25)*

Clearly 'covenant' must be very important to God for it to be so closely identified with the sacrifice Jesus made on the Cross. This raises a number of questions: What is a covenant? When did God establish the old covenant? What are the differences between the old and the new covenant? What does it mean for Christians today to be part of this covenant?

Essentially a covenant is a contract, a pledge, a treaty, a binding oath or agreement. Throughout the Old Testament God made a series of covenants: with His creation, with the nation of Israel, with certain individuals. He gave His word to do, and not to do, certain things promises, He would never break. **He would always remain faithful to the covenant pledges He made and would not revoke anything he had promised.**

Because God made these covenants within the context of His relationship with His people, He often required certain things of them including obedience to His commands. So a covenant became an agreement between God and His people. He promised to bless them in certain ways, if they obeyed the commands He gave them. He was under no obligation to fulfil the promises if the people disobeyed these commands.

THE TERMS OF ANY COVENANT GOD MADE WITH HIS PEOPLE IS DETERMINED BY HIM ALONE.

Behind every covenant is God's desire to bless His people and provide for them. Obedience would bring prosperity; disobedience would result in curse rather than His intended blessings.

The terms of any covenant God made with His people is determined by Him alone. Men cannot sit down with the Lord and work out an agreement with Him. The initiative is entirely His. (He never *needed* to enter into a covenant; He chose to do so.) Knowing He would always remain faithful to every word He spoke, God was not afraid to do this. Although His people assented again and again to the terms of the covenants He placed before them, they consistently failed to fulfil their covenant obligations.

They often became disobedient in times of blessing and prosperity. Having all they desired, they no longer felt the need to depend on the Lord. Even though He warned them of the consequences of disobedience, they would at first compromise and then drift right away from God's will. This brought about the curses God wanted them to avoid: defeat, bondage, famine and devastation. When they repented, they once again embraced God and sought to obey their covenant responsibilities. As soon as they obeyed His commands, they prospered again.

However, God was looking forward to the establishing of the new covenant that would enable His people to have an entirely new and different relationship with Him, in which they would be able to enjoy His blessings continually.

At the heart of covenant is the often stated promise: "I will be *your* God, and you shall be *my* people." Your God; my people. A covenant people are those who belong to God. This speaks of a deep lasting relationship, which the Lord desires to have with His beloved ones.

He has made it possible for you to have such a relationship, in which He blesses you with abundant grace, supplying your every need now and giving you the promise of an eternity spent with Him in His glory.

... HE BLESSES YOU WITH ABUNDANT GRACE, SUPPLYING YOUR EVERY NEED NOW AND GIVING YOU THE PROMISE OF AN ETERNITY SPENT WITH HIM IN HIS GLORY.

Before looking at what is involved in the new covenant established through the blood of Christ, we will consider briefly the concept of covenant in the Old Testament, for by doing this we can learn about how to relate to God in covenant.

God chose to make covenants with His people because:

• He wanted a people who would be loyal, faithful and obedient to Him, so that He could bless Him.

- His people needed to know what He expected of them in order to receive this flow of blessing He desired to impart to them.

- He wanted to help them to remain faithful to Him; and so be able to receive His abundant prosperity.

- He wanted their prosperity to be a witness to other nations that He is the true God.

2

COVENANT IN THE
OLD TESTAMENT

NOAH

The devastation of the Flood signified the judgement mankind deserved because of his sin:

> *Then the LORD saw that the wickedness of man was great in the earth, and that every intent of the thoughts of his heart was only evil continually. (Genesis 6: 5 NKJ)*

Yet God made a covenant with Noah, promising him salvation! He would save him and his family from the devastation of the flood because he walked righteously before the Lord.

After the flood, God made a covenant with the whole of creation. He made a solemn oath that He would never revoke:

> *Then the LORD said in His heart, "I will never again curse the ground for man's sake, although the imagination of man's heart is evil from his youth; nor will I again destroy every living thing as I have done." (Genesis 8: 21 NKJ)*

So God said to Noah:

*I establish my covenant with you: Never again will
all be cut off by the waters of the flood; never again will there be a
flood to destroy the earth. (Genesis 9: 11)*

God then chose to make the rainbow a sign of His covenant:

*I have set my rainbow in the clouds, and it shall be for the sign of
the covenant between me and the earth. (Genesis 9: 13)*

ABRAHAM

God spoke to Abraham of the wonderful ways in which He would
bless him. These promises are very important, for they speak of
God's purpose for making covenant with His
people; He wanted to bless them, not judge
them. He wanted them to prosper, not be
under condemnation. Later we shall see that
there is a direct link between the covenant
promises made to Abraham, and what God
accomplished in the establishing of the New
Covenant. He said to Abram:

> BEING IN A COVENANT
> RELATIONSHIP WITH
> GOD PLACES US UNDER
> HIS PROTECTION!

*I will make you a great nation; I will bless you and make your
name great; and you shall be a blessing. I will bless those who
bless you, and I will curse him who curses you; and in you all the
families of the earth shall be blessed. (Genesis 12: 2-3)*

**Being in a covenant relationship with God, not only places us
in the flow of His blessings, but also under His protection!** The

Lord actually appeared to Abraham when He made the covenant with him, and said:

> *I am Almighty God; walk before Me and be blameless.*
> *And I will make My covenant between Me and you,*
> *and will multiply you exceedingly…As for Me, behold,*
> *My covenant is with you, and you shall be a father of*
> *many nations. (Genesis 17: 1-2, 4 NKJ)*

Although the covenant was made with Abram personally, it would pass to successive generations:

> *And I will establish My covenant between Me and you*
> *and your descendants after you in their generations,*
> *for an everlasting covenant, to be God to you and your*
> *descendants after you. (Genesis 17: 7 NKJ)*

Circumcision was to be the sign of this covenant, a sign that they must not put their trust in the flesh but in their covenant God. It was the sign of a people belonging to God, His people whom He could bless. It was also to be a sign of their obedience to Him, of their submission to His authority as their Lord. In the New Covenant there would be a different kind of circumcision!

MOSES

To Moses God gave the covenant law to pass onto the nation. Before the deliverance from Egypt, the Lord had reminded Moses of the covenant already established with Abraham, Sarah and Jacob – to give them the Promised Land. To fulfil that covenant promise, He will deliver His people from their bondage under Pharaoh; for everything God does in relation to His people is to fulfil His covenant word to them! He repeats to Moses the covenant truth of belonging:

> *I will take you as My people, and I will be your God.*
> *Then you shall know that I am the LORD your God who brings*
> *you out from under the burdens of the Egyptians.*
> *And I will bring you into the land which I swore to give to*
> *Abraham, Isaac, and Jacob; and I will give it to you*
> *as a heritage: I am the LORD. (Exodus 6: 7-8 NKJ)*

After their deliverance God gave the people the covenant law, centered around the Ten Commandments. Deuteronomy 28 sets out clearly the blessings He promised the people whenever they obey their covenant obligations; and the curses they will bring on themselves through disobedience.

> *If you diligently obey the voice of the LORD your God,*
> *to observe carefully all His commandments which I command*
> *you today, then the LORD your God will set you high*
> *above all the nations of the earth. And all these blessings*
> *shall come upon you and overtake you, because you obey*
> *the voice of the LORD your God.*
> *(Deuteronomy 28: 1-2 NKJ)*

They will be blessed in the city and in the country. Their crops and herds will prosper and increase. They will be blessed when they come in and go out. They will see their enemies defeated. They will be established as a holy people, trusting in the Lord and set apart for His purposes! They will prosper in every conceivable way:

And the LORD will make you the head and not the tail;
you shall be above only, and not be beneath,
if you heed the commandments of the LORD your God.
(Deuteronomy 28: 13 NKJ)

The need of obedience is repeated again and again. And when God later renewed the covenant at Moab, He again emphasised the need to obey:

Therefore keep the words of this covenant, and do them,
that you may prosper in all that you do…enter into covenant
with the LORD your God, and into His oath, which the LORD
your God makes with you today, that He may establish you today as
a people for Himself. (Deuteronomy 29: 9, 12-13 NKJ)

Sadly, during their subsequent history, the people fell into disobedience again and again, thus bringing on themselves the curses about which God had warned them. **Yet every time they turned back to Him in repentance, He restored their relationship with Himself and renewed their prosperity.**

We will see that obedience has a significant part to play in the outworking of the New Covenant in our lives!

DAVID

As well as the covenant with the nation, God also made covenants with certain individuals. As an example we will take the covenant He made with David. The Lord promised David that his own "seed" would succeed him as king, and that his son would "build a house for My name." Solomon fulfilled these promises.

Of greater significance was the promise that the Messiah would come from his lineage:

And your house and your kingdom shall be established forever before you. Your throne shall be established forever.
(2 Samuel 7: 16 NKJ)

In Psalm 59, David speaks prophetically of the Messianic promise. Again, God emphasises that He will remain faithful to His oath, to His covenant words of promise, by saying:

My covenant I will not break, nor alter the word that has gone out of My lips. Once I have sworn by My holiness; I will not lie to David: His seed shall endure forever. (Psalm 89: 34-36 NKJ)

All this is pointing forward prophetically to the New Covenant that is to be established by Jesus, the Messiah.

3

A NEW COVENANT NEEDED

JEREMIAH

God speaks through the prophet Jeremiah to state the nature of the New Covenant, which will be radically different from the old one, not in intention, but in the way God's purposes will be fulfilled. Instead of the law being written on stone tablets or codified in a book, God says:

> *I will put My law in their minds, and write it on their hearts;*
> *and I will be their God, and they shall be My people.*
> *(Jeremiah 31: 33 NKJ)*

There is a restating that the purpose of the covenant is relationship, that He will be their God, and they His people. They will *belong*.

Obedience will also be expected by the Lord, but not an external obedience to written law, but an obedience that comes from the heart, from a genuine desire to please the One to whom they belong as a people! This relationship, this sense of belonging, will be for every individual who is part of this New Covenant:

No more shall every man teach his neighbour, and every man his brother, saying, 'Know the Lord,' for they shall all know Me, from the least of them to the greatest of them, says the LORD. For I will forgive their iniquity, and their sin I will remember no more. (Jeremiah 31: 34 NKJ)

THIS SACRIFICE WOULD MAKE IT POSSIBLE FOR PEOPLE TO BE RECONCILED TO GOD, TO BE MADE ONE WITH HIM, AND TO ENTER INTO AN ETERNAL COVENANT WITH HIM.

To establish this New Covenant, the people would need forgiveness. They could not be 'at one' with God while in a state of sin, which brings about spiritual death. A blameless life would have to be made as a sacrifice on behalf of the guilty. It would be ratified, therefore, with a sacrifice of blood, making it necessary for Jesus to be the Lamb of God, the sacrifice provided by God Himself, the Lamb without blemish. The sacrifice of the Sinless One was made for sinners, the Holy One for the unholy, the Perfect for the imperfect, the totally obedient One for the disobedient.

This sacrifice would make it possible for people to be reconciled to God, to be made one with Him, and to enter into an eternal covenant with Him.

EZEKIEL

The Lord spoke through Ezekiel to say what He would do when this New Covenant was established:

I will cleanse you from all your filthiness and from all your idols.

I will give you a new heart and put a new spirit within you;
I will take the heart of stone out of your flesh and give you a heart
of flesh. I will put My spirit within you and cause you
to walk in My statutes, and you will keep My judgements
and do them. (Ezekiel 36: 25-27 NKJ)

The emphasis is on what the Lord will do when He establishes the New Covenant. Again He reiterates the promise of being His own people, who will enter into the inheritance promised them:

Then you shall dwell in the land that I gave
to your fathers; you shall be My people and I will be
your God. (Ezekiel 36: 28 NKJ)

God describes this as "a covenant of peace." He promises to establish "an everlasting covenant." First atonement for their sins will have to be made, to cleanse them and make it possible for them to be drawn into a lasting relationship with Him, instead of one that was continually being broken through their disobedience.

ISAIAH

To the prophet Isaiah, God speaks of His "servant." This refers to the people He sets apart for Himself; then to the faithful remnant among these people; then finally to Jesus, the One who would become the Suffering Servant. Throughout these messages about the servant, God speaks of covenant. We can understand these statements as referring to Jesus, to those who are faithful to Him, and to His desire for all His people: The Lord says:

I, the LORD, have called you in righteousness; I will take
hold of your hand. I will keep you and will make you to be a
covenant for the people and a light for the Gentiles, to open eyes that
are blind, to free captives from prison and to release form the
dungeon those who sit in darkness. (Isaiah 42: 6-7)

Here we can detect the intimate nature of the relationship God wants to establish with His covenant people. We see also the immense fruit that will result from covenant. Not only will His people be blessed but many others will be touched by the power of God working in and through His people.

This is what the LORD says: "In the time of favour
I will answer you, and in the day of salvation I will help you;
I will keep you and will make you to be a covenant for the people,
to restore the land." (Isaiah 49:8)

God has a covenant people that He might live in and among them, that He might express the life of His Kingdom in their lives and so bring spiritual reformation to the nations. He promises His people:

"Yet my unfailing love for you will not be shaken
nor my covenant of peace be removed," says the LORD,
who has compassion on you. (Isaiah 54:10)

Those who are faithful to Him will hold fast to the covenant and will be those He can use effectively to fulfil His purposes. He speaks of the New Covenant that will be established in the power of the Holy Spirit, and will pass on from generation to generation among those who love Him:

"As for me, this is my covenant with them," says the LORD.
"My Spirit, who is on you, and my words that I have put in your
mouth will not depart from your mouth, or from the mouths of your
children, or from the mouths of their descendants from this time
on forever," says the LORD. (Isaiah 59:21)

It is, then, *"an everlasting covenant." (Isaiah 61:8)*

It is clear that for centuries God was preparing to establish the New
Covenant. He was longing for the time when it would be right to
send His Son to do all that was necessary to draw His people into
this close relationship, in which they could become one with Him
and His sovereign purposes.

4

JESUS: MEDIATOR OF THE NEW COVENANT

Jesus lived in a covenant relationship with His Father; He and the Father were One in every way. **This unity made it possible for us to become One with Him, receive His Spirit and be those through whom He could speak His word to the world.** All this was accomplished by establishing the New Covenant.

> *He is also Mediator of a better covenant, which was established on better promises. (Hebrews 8: 6 NKJ)*

Before His birth, Zacharias, the father of John the Baptist, prophesied about Jesus, the coming Messiah. God was sending His Son:

> *To perform the mercy promised to our fathers and to remember His holy covenant, the oath which He swore to our father Abraham: To grant us that we, being delivered from the hand of our enemies, might serve Him without fear, in holiness and righteousness before Him all the days of our life. (Luke 1: 72-75 NKJ)*

As a result of the New Covenant, we would be delivered out of the power of our enemies, the devil and all his works. We will be free to serve God in love, without fear. Those belonging to the New Covenant will be able to live as a holy people, set-apart for God's purposes, enjoying the life of righteousness that is His gift to all who put their faith in Jesus.

A NEW AND BETTER COVENANT WAS NEEDED BECAUSE GOD'S PEOPLE FAILED TO KEEP THE FORMER ONE;

They would receive, not a Promised Land on this earth, but, *"the promise of the eternal inheritance," (Hebrews 9: 15)* that God wants for His new covenant people. So Jesus became the guarantee of *"a better covenant." (Hebrews 7: 22)*

A new and better covenant was needed because God's people failed to keep the former one; they constantly broke covenant with Him. **Now with new hearts and His Holy Spirit living within them, they would be able to obey His commands and maintain their unity with Him.**

Even under the Old Covenant, God had promised to forgive His people. They could not make themselves right with God and forgive their own sins, which had the effect of separating them from God, breaking fellowship with Him. One of the purposes of the old sacrificial system was to bring to God an offering of blood, symbolising life, to atone for the sins of the people. The word 'atone' means 'at one.' The purpose of the sacrifice was to restore their relationship with God, making it possible to be at one with Him.

God had always wanted to dwell among His people. First in the tabernacle in the wilderness, then in the Temple in Jerusalem. The Holy of holies was the dwelling place of God among His chosen people. This place was so sacred that no one was allowed to enter it except the High Priest, and he only once a year on the Day of Atonement, carrying the blood of animals offered for his own sins and for those of the people. Of course this sacrifice had to be repeated every year.

On the Mount of Transfiguration Jesus' mortal body was changed into a glorious body. Because He had not committed any sin He could have simply returned to heaven at that point; He already belonged to the glory. If He had done so, He could not have taken any 'sinners' with Him. So He came down the mountain and set His face to go deliberately to Jerusalem, knowing that there He would become the perfect sacrifice made on behalf of all sinners, the Lamb of God sent to take away the sins of the world.

HIS SACRIFICE WOULD NEVER HAVE TO BE REPEATED; IT WOULD 'ATONE' FOR THE SINS OF ALL MANKIND OF EVERY GENERATION.

So Jesus was to become not only the sacrifice, but the High Priest who entered the sanctuary of heaven, the Holy of holies, the dwelling place of God. He 'carried' His own blood, not that of animals. **His sacrifice would never have to be repeated; it would 'atone' for the sins of all mankind of every generation. All who put their faith in Jesus could be made 'at one' with God.**

So He is the High Priest of this new and better covenant. The letter to the Hebrews gives us wonderful insights into what this means.

To know Jesus as your High Priest will enable you to live a life of faith, knowing that God wants to bless you continually and to answer your prayers.

It is best to read the whole of this epistle in a good modern translation, for it is not a particularly easy book to understand. Here we can focus on some of the key points that will help you understand what it means to know Jesus is *now* your High Priest. You will probably be amazed to see what He is doing on your behalf right now in Heaven!

5

OUR HIGH PRIEST IN HEAVEN

The opening chapters of Hebrews speak of Jesus becoming man to effect God's purposes here on earth. Chapter 3 begins:

> *Therefore, holy brothers, who share in the heavenly calling,*
> *fix your thoughts on Jesus, the apostle and high priest*
> *whom we confess. (Hebrews 3: 1)*

This epistle is addressed to the Christian community generally and the writer describes his readers as 'holy brothers' – those who are set apart for God, having been forgiven and made pure in His sight. They share a "heavenly calling." Not only can they look forward to the glory of heaven, but they are called to live the life of God's heavenly Kingdom here on earth.

The readers are urged to fix their thoughts on Jesus, first as Apostle, and then as High Priest. An apostle is one who is sent to fulfil a specific purpose. Jesus made it clear repeatedly that the Father *sent* Him. He would become, not only the sacrifice offered on our part on the cross to enable us to be 'at one' with God; He was also sent to be our High Priest, who would return to heaven carrying that blood on our behalf enabling us to enter the Holy of holies, not a sanctuary in an earthly building, but the sanctuary of God's Presence in heaven.

> *Therefore, since we have a great high priest, who has gone through the heavens, Jesus the Son of God, let us hold firmly to the faith we profess. (Hebrews 4:14)*

Moses was used by God to inaugurate the Old Covenant, but Jesus the new and better covenant. Receiving Jesus as our High Priest is going to make a great difference to the level of faith expressed in our lives now!

> *For we do not have a high priest who is unable to sympathise with our weaknesses, but we have one who has been tempted in every way, just as we are — yet was without sin. (Hebrews 4:15)*

Jesus came and identified completely with us in our weaknesses, sharing our humanity completely, yet without ever falling into sin! The One who would be our High Priest had to be able to represent us; so He had to become one of us.

Because He offered up the perfect sacrifice for us, He has opened up the way into the Holy of holies for us. We are able to come before God's throne now. For believers this is not a throne of judgement, but the throne of grace. So the writer urges us:

> *Let us then approach the throne of grace with confidence so that we may receive mercy and find grace to help us in our time of need. (Hebrews 4: 16)*

When we confess our sins, that mercy ensures our forgiveness and full acceptance by God. He does not hold forgiven sin against us.

It is easy to receive grace, for this is what God gives to those who deserve nothing! So we do not approach God's throne in prayer, worrying whether we of ourselves deserve anything, but **knowing that God wants to bless us abundantly as those who belong to the New Covenant, because now we are identified completely with our High Priest in heaven, just as He is identified completely with us on earth.** How can this be?

> GOD WANTS TO BLESS US ABUNDANTLY AS ... WE ARE IDENTIFIED COMPLETELY WITH OUR HIGH PRIEST IN HEAVEN

The writer emphasises the purpose of a high priest:

> *Every high priest is selected from among men and is appointed to represent them in matters related to God, to offer gifts and sacrifices for sins. (Hebrew 5: 1)*

As our High Priest, sent by God, Jesus now represents us, not on earth but in heaven, in matters related to God. As *your* High Priest He represents *you* before God the Father. He has offered to the Father the gift of His blood on *your* behalf; He has sacrificed Himself for *your* forgiveness and acceptance, making it possible for *you* to have a new life 'at one' with God. *[Jesus entered heaven 'on our behalf.' (Hebrews 6: 20)]* So what is He doing in heaven now on your behalf?

Unlike the high priests of the old order who had to offer sacrifice for their own sins as well as those of the people, our High Priest was able to enter to heaven itself and there He lives in *"the power of an indestructible life,"* *(Hebrews 7: 16)* the eternal life He gives to all who turn to Him with repentance and faith.

> *Therefore he is able to save completely those who come to God through him, because he always lives to intercede for them. (Hebrews 7: 25)*

He saves you completely. This is a continual process. He lives to save you from sin, from sickness, deception, the power of the devil. He lives to save you for God's purposes, to make it possible to fulfil His purpose for you on earth. There cannot be a need in your life that is not covered by His intercession, as He holds that blood continually before the Father for you.

> *Such a high priest meets our need – one who is holy, blameless, pure, set apart from sinners, exalted above the heavens. (Hebrews 7: 26)*

He is now in heaven interceding for you – in the power of an indestructible, eternal life!

We do not have such a high priest, who sat down at the right hand of the throne of the Majesty in heaven, and who serves in the sanctuary, the true tabernacle set up by the Lord, not by man. (Hebrews 8: 1-2)

Having accomplished on earth all He was sent to do; having offered His life as the perfect sacrifice, Jesus is now seated in glory in heaven. However, He is not idle; He lives to "serve in the sanctuary."

We are used to thinking of Jesus coming to earth as the Suffering Servant. He served the people as He taught about the Kingdom, healed the sick, raised the dead and performed many other miracles out of His compassion and love, demonstrating the power and authority of God's Kingdom on earth.

Yet most Christians speak as if His servant days ended after He had offered His life on the cross and subsequently ascended to heaven. Not according to God's Word!

Jesus lives to serve in the heavenly sanctuary now. After all, He said that the greatest in the Kingdom is the servant of all! **He reigns in heaven** *now,* **serving us in the power of an indestructible and sinless life** *now,* **representing us before the Father** *now,* **interceding for us and dispersing His heavenly life to all who believe in Him** *now!*

Do you see what this means? Jesus not only comes to earth *for you;* He lives in heaven *for you!* He wants to serve you continually in the power of His indestructible life to meet every one of your needs, *"according to his riches in glory." (Philippians 4:19)*

> *He entered heaven itself, now to appear for us in*
> *God's presence. (Hebrews 9: 24)*

He is in heaven for you, just as He came to earth for you! What wonderful truth! Even there He wants to continue to serve you with His eternal, indestructible life! No wonder the writer says:

> *Therefore, brothers, since we have confidence to enter the Most*
> *Holy Place by the blood of Jesus, by a new and living way opened for*

us through the curtain, that is, his body, and since we have a great priest over the house of God, let us draw near to God with a sincere heart in full assurance of faith. (Hebrews 10: 19-22)

We can have bold faith to draw near to God in the name of the One who represents us before God. We can stand confidently before His throne of grace, expecting to receive from Him through the One who intercedes for us and serves us in the power of His indestructible life!

Paul says that we have peace with God through Jesus, *"though whom we have gained access by faith into this grace in which we now stand." (Romans 5: 2)* The significance of this is immense:

And God is able to make all grace abound to you, so that in all things at all times, having all that you need, you will abound in every good work. (2 Corinthians 9: 8)

6

NOW YOU CAN PROSPER

God certainly wants you to prosper in every way. As you seek first His Kingdom, (His reign in your life) and to live in righteousness, (at one with Him) He will add everything you need. This is one of the New Covenant promises Jesus gives. You do not need to worry about anything! **Your High Priest in heaven will be with you always by His Spirit; He will watch over you, provide for you and give you all the grace you need to enable you to fulfil His purpose on earth.**

YOUR HIGH PRIEST IN HEAVEN WILL BE WITH YOU ALWAYS BY HIS SPIRIT; HE WILL WATCH OVER YOU ...

This is the greatness of the New Covenant established through the blood of Jesus! As a believer in Him, you are part of that covenant. All the promises of both the old and the new covenants are yours! God wants to bless you and prosper you in every way to fulfil His plan and purpose for your life. No wonder the writer to Hebrews urges us:

> *Let us throw off everything that hinders and the sin that*
> *so easily entangles, and let us run with perseverance*
> *the race marked out for us. (Hebrews 12: 1)*

Why allow anything to hinder your relationship with God, when Jesus has made it possible for you to be 'at one' with him? **You are no longer in bondage to sin. You are a saint, a holy brother or sister, set apart for God's purposes! You can persevere in a life of faith, expecting that Jesus will continually dispense His life to you from heaven.** He does this through His Spirit who lives in you.

When you understand and appreciate this, it makes all the difference to your prayer life. Prayer is not boring, or a legalistic routine or duty. It is vibrant, full of life and expectation, because you draw near to the throne of grace and meet with your High Priest. Jesus knew what the effect of His sacrifice would be. This is why, as part of the New Covenant, He gives such wonderful promises concerning prayer.

> *And I will do whatever you ask in my name, so that the*
> *Son may bring glory to the Father. You may ask me for anything*
> *in my name, and I will do it. (John 14: 13-14)*

To pray in the name of Jesus means far more than using His name when praying. It is to pray conscious that you have **One in heaven who represents you before the Father, who intercedes with His all-powerful blood, who is willing to serve you in the power of His indestructible life.**

In other words, He lives to give Himself to us eternally. He has purposed good things for us to walk in. He "has blessed us in the heavenly realms with every spiritual blessing in Christ" (Ephesians 1: 3). He wants us therefore to lay hold of those blessings by faith in His grace, in His desire to give to us although we deserve nothing!

If you remain in me, and my words remain in you,
ask whatever you wish, and it will be given you.
(John 15: 7)

What an amazing promise: *"Anything you wish"!* Is Jesus really serious? Certainly! He knew that if you live in Him, and His word in you, you will not ask for anything to serve your flesh. He will meet very practical needs in very practical ways, by releasing His power from heaven into your life and circumstances He is overseeing your life from heaven!

Faith is not trying to persuade God to do things for you; it is living in a relationship with God through Jesus, a relationship in which you know He wants to give to you all that is good and right. He never wants to give to His covenant children anything that would harm them. Even when He needs to discipline them it is always in love as a father disciplines the children he loves, for their good!

And so the writer to Hebrews tells us, not only to throw off everything that is a hindrance to that faith relationship; he also urges:

Let us fix our eyes on Jesus, the author and perfecter of our faith,
who for the joy set before him endured the cross, scorning its shame,
and sat down at the right hand of the throne of God.
Consider him … (Hebrews 12: 2-3)

At that place at the right hand of the Father, He continually represents you, intercedes for you and serves you in the power of His heavenly life!

Consider Him! Consider Him! Consider Him! When Jesus taught His disciples how to pray with faith, the first thing He said was: *"Have faith in God." (Mark 11: 22)* This sounds such a simple statement that it is easy to miss its significance. Jesus is in effect saying: let your faith be in God, not in your faith! It is not a matter of trusting in the words you pray or in your faith. Trust in the One to whom you pray, the One who is now in heaven for you, who wants to serve you and give to you.

You will not be heard for your many words, Jesus warns. Neither can you reduce a relationship of faith with God through Jesus Christ, to a series of formulae and faith confessions, useful though they are!

Your faith is to be in God, to whom you have direct access through the One who is now your High Priest in heaven. **Consider Him! Consider Him! Consider Him!**

Consider what he has already done for you in sacrificing His own blood for you. Consider the great ways in which He has already to you. Having forgiven your sins and made you acceptable to God, He had given you His eternal life, making you indestructible! He has put His Kingdom within you and has given you His own Holy Spirit.

Yes, consider all He has done for you, and all He has given you. But consider also who He is now: your High Priest in heaven, dispensing to you all the blessings of the New Covenant to which you belong through His mercy, grace and love for you!

7

MINISTERS OF A NEW COVENANT

Because you belong to the New Covenant, you are a minister of this covenant!

Paul, the apostle, was a very able man. However, he learned that serving God in his own human wisdom, understanding and abilities, led to him denying Jesus and persecuting the Church. That is the result of trying to please God through religious formalism!

When he met with the ascended Jesus on the road to Damascus, he not only experienced a dramatic conversion; he came to a complete re-evaluation of his human abilities. He came to see the truth of Jesus' words that apart from Him we can do nothing! Anything that does not stem from faith in Jesus and dependence on Him, is worth nothing in God's eyes. Therefore Paul tells the Corinthians:

> *Such confidence as this is ours through Christ before God.*
> *Not that we are competent in ourselves to claim anything*
> *or ourselves, but our competence comes from God.*
> *(2 Corinthians 3: 4-5)*

We have seen how Jesus makes it possible for us to have confidence before God. This is not because of anything we have done, but is based on what Jesus has done and continues to do for us as our High Priest! Our competence, our ability comes from God.

JESUS LIVES IN HEAVEN AND CONTINUES TO SERVE US IN THE POWER OF HIS HEAVENLY LIFE THROUGH OUR RELATIONSHIP OF FAITH IN HIM.

Jesus lives in heaven and continues to serve us in the power of His heavenly life through our relationship of faith in Him. He is the Author and Perfecter of our faith because He lived in perfect faith and dependence on His Father while He was on earth! He made it clear that, although He was the Word who had become man, He spoke no words of His own, but only the words His Father gave Him to speak.

The Father served Him from heaven, just as Jesus serves us now! He said He could do nothing of Himself, but only the works He saw his Father doing; He had not come to do His own will but the will of His Father who sent Him. He did not live for Himself, but had come to lay down His life for His friends! His works were in reality the works of His Father done through Him.

Such dependence on God, meant Jesus could say, "the Father and I are one!" (John 10: 30) Yet at the same time: "The Father is greater than I." (John 14: 28) He lived in complete dependence on the Father, submitting to Him in all things.

Through our relationship of faith and dependence on Jesus, we are able to be ministers of the New Covenant. **He is able to minister**

this heavenly life through us. Just as the Father was able to work through Jesus, so Jesus is now able to work through us. Paul says:

> *He has made us competent as ministers of a new covenant –*
> *not of the letter but of the Spirit; for the letter kills, but*
> *the Spirit gives life. (2 Corinthians 3: 6)*

Not only does He channel His grace to us, but *through* us to others. Not only does He love us; we are to love one another. John, the apostle, says:

> *This is the message you heard from the beginning:*
> *We should love one another. (1 John 3: 11)*

The New Covenant is a covenant of love: the love Jesus has shown us on the cross: the love He pours out upon us now as He serves us from heaven as our great High Priest. And the love those who belong to the New Covenant are to show to one another.

> *This is how we know what love is: Jesus Christ laid down*
> *his life for us. And we ought to lay down our lives for our*
> *brothers. (1 John 3: 16)*

We have seen how essential obedience is to the whole understanding of covenant. Jesus wants us to bless us abundantly from heaven through His great love. A relationship of faith in Him has to be a relationship of love for Him. And Jesus made clear:

> *As the Father has loved me, so have I loved you. Now remain*
> *in my love. If you obey my commands you will remain in my love,*
> *just as I obeyed my Father's commands and remain in His love.*
> *(John 15: 9-10)*

To remain at one with His Father, Jesus had to live in obedience to Him! One act of disobedience and He could not have been our sacrifice for sin, neither could He have become our High Priest in heaven ministering to us in the power of an indestructible, eternal life!

To enable Him to inaugurate the New Covenant, He had to live in obedience to His Father. Under the old covenant, God's people continually failed through their disobedience. Under the new God made it possible for His people to obey Him, not out of slavish subservience but out of love. Such a covenant could only be established through One who was Himself obedient in every respect. **Under the New Covenant God chose to write His law, His words of covenant, not on tablets of stone but on the hearts of all those who turn to Him in repentance and faith. At the same time He placed His own Spirit within them to enable them to keep those commands.**

Whenever we fail to obey, we have the blood of Jesus available to cleanse us from our sins and restore us to a relationship of righteousness with God. However, this should not give us a casual attitude towards sin, as if it does not matter too much because we can rely on God's forgiveness! Such an attitude makes it clear there is a definite lack of love for Jesus! Those who love Him obey His commands!

8

THE CHURCH:
A COVENANT PEOPLE

With the New Covenant comes a new command. Under the old one we are to love God with all our heart, mind, soul and strength. We are to love our neighbours as ourselves. This is still God's purpose. Jesus added a new command to these, the command distinctive of the New Covenant:

> *A new command I give you: Love one another.*
> *As I have loved you, so you must love one another.*
> *By this all men will know that you are my disciples,*
> *if you love one another. (John 13: 34-35)*

Our great High Priest continues to serve us from heaven, pouring His love into our hearts by the Holy Spirit. In effect He tells us that this love is to flow to one another as those who are His covenant children. **The Church is to be a body of people living in covenant unity with their Lord in heaven; and in covenant love for one another.**

At first, this seems an inward-looking approach for the Church.

However, obedience is better than sacrifice! We will accomplish far more by obeying what Jesus tells us to do than be involved in sacrificial activity that is not His will or command to us.

OUR UNITY WITH ONE ANOTHER IS TO BE A REFLECTION OF THE UNITY BETWEEN THE FATHER AND THE SON.

And God is infinitely wiser than we are. He knows that such a body of people living in covenant love for Him and for one another, will be far more effective in communicating the gospel of the Kingdom to the world. This is why Jesus prayed for all who would come to believe in Him, by saying:

> *I pray also for those who will believe in me through this message, that all of them may be one, Father, just as you are one in me and I am in you. May they also be in us so that the world may believe that you have sent me. I have given them the glory you gave me, that they may be one as we are one: I in them and you in me. May they be brought to complete unity to let the world know that you sent me and have loved them even as you have loved me. (John 17: 20-23)*

Through this extraordinary prayer, it is wonderful to know that Jesus was praying for us, those who would come to believe in Him through the apostles' message. It is even more wonderful to see what He prayed.

Our unity with Him is such that we live in Him and He in us.

Our unity with one another is to be a reflection of the unity between the Father and the Son.

Clearly, Jesus is not talking about structural church unity between different denominations, but about relationship. Because of all Jesus has done as our High Priest we can be totally at one with Him as part of the New Covenant. Our love for one another cannot be superficial or temporary. **If our relationships with each other reflect the unity between the Father and Son, then they will be wholehearted and lasting!**

The New Covenant is expressed then, not only in our love for God, but in the unity we have with one another, the way in which we love our brothers and sisters in Christ. **Jesus promises that the effect of this is that the world will believe, because the unsaved will see such an amazing quality of love among believers.** This is love that will draw people into the Kingdom, into the new covenant community of love. And this is what any local expression of the Body of Christ is to be, ministers of the New Covenant, first to one another, then to the world.

At the Last Supper, Jesus said that those who loved Him would obey His commands, and so live in the fullness of God's love. The joy of Jesus will be in them and their joy will be full. He then says:

> *My command is this: Love one another as I have loved you.*
> *Greater love has no man than this, that he lay down*
> *his life or his friends. You are my friends if you do*
> *what I command. (John 15: 12-14)*

We are to love one another in the same way that He loved us. He loved us by laying His life down for us; so we are to love one another by laying down our lives for our friends. This will make us friends of Jesus.

This, then, is the meaning of covenant love: to lay down your life for others. Jesus was able to remain in the Father's love because He lay down His life. He said:

> *The reason my Father loves me is that I lay down my life.*
> *(John 10:17)*

And this is how we shall remain in the love of Jesus; by obediently laying down our lives for one another in love. Such love has nothing to do with sentiment or emotion; it is God's law, expressed in giving of yourself to others. The church is often so weak in her witness to the world because such love is lacking. No wonder Paul said:

> *If I speak in the tongues of men and of angels,*
> *but have not love, I am only a resounding gong or a clanging*
> *symbol. If I have the gift of prophecy and can fathom*
> *all mysteries and all knowledge, and if I have a faith*
> *that can move mountains, but have not love, I am nothing.*
> *(1 Corinthians 13: 1-2)*

Nothing can compensate for a lack of this covenant love, no matter how anointed or gifted a believer, or how strong his or her faith. Such a believer is nothing without such love! John says:

> *Dear children, let us not love with words or tongue*
> *but with action and in truth. (1 John 3: 18)*

Some Christians can be very good at telling others that they love them, and even giving them a hug, but without doing anything for them or giving to them in any other way. John is clear: let us not love like that. **True love has to be expressed in action!** In the same way, James says that faith has to be expressed in deeds:

> *What good is it, my brothers, if a man claims to have*
> *faith but has no deeds? (James 2: 14)*

It is clear that the New Testament (or covenant) writers have no time for super-spiritual talk and no action! Those who say the right things, but have no loving deeds to back up their words are self-deceived and live in spiritual unreality. Both love and faith are to be real, not only a matter of talking! So John says:

> *Dear friends, let us love one another, for love comes from God.*
> *Everyone who loved has been born of God and knows God.*
> *(1 John 4: 7)*

The one who only speaks love deceives himself about his relationship with God and his usefulness to others.

> *For anyone who does not love his brother, whom he has seen,*
> *cannot love God, whom he has not seen. And he has given us*
> *this command: Whoever loves God must also love*
> *his brother. (1 John 4: 20-21)*

The biblical evidence is clear. Our love for God is not real unless we are laying down our lives for others. **This is not extreme; it is what New Testament believers were taught from the beginning of their Christian experience.** This is what it means to belong to Jesus as part of the New Covenant he brought into being by laying down His life for us!

9

THE NATURE OF TRUE LOVE

Paul gives us a wonderful description of the true nature of God's love. This is the love that was expressed in the ministry of Jesus, that He has for every one of us, and that is to be expressed in our relationships with one another. For we are to love one another with the same love with which He has loved us!

Love is patient, love is kind. It does not envy, it does not boast, it is not proud. It is not rude, it is not self-seeking, it is not easily angered, it keeps no record of wrongs. Love does not delight in evil but rejoices with the truth. It always protects, always trusts, always hopes, always perseveres. Love never fails. (1 Corinthians 13: 4-8)

This is the love of God that is to be expressed in every believer. This is only possible if you have a right heart attitude towards other Christians, especially those with whom you are immediately involved. Anyone who is serious about his or her covenant responsibilities to others, will seek to have the following heart attitudes:

A) Patience. God is continually merciful and patient with us; and so we are to act likewise towards others. If we judge others we will easily become impatient with them. Better to thank God that He is so patient with you and to concentrate on getting the outworking of love right in your life, than in criticising others for failing to do so.

B) Kind. This is to be expressed in the loving way in which we serve others. It is the expression of a heart like that of Jesus: "gentle and humble." Kindness is not only an attitude, but is expressed in the kind deeds we do for others.

C) Does Not Envy. If you love others you will rejoice with them when they are blessed and when they prosper. The One who blesses them will bless you; so you do not need to be envious. Instead, be happy for them because of the way they prosper, as you would anyone you truly love.

D) It Does Not Boast. Those who walk in the flesh talk constantly about themselves, draw attention to themselves and want others to know about their exploits! Those who love are humble because they are concerned about the welfare of others rather than their own pride.

E) It is Not Proud. The proud think they are better than other believers, more anointed, more gifted, more spiritual even. Such attitudes are the result of a proud heart, something God hates!

F) It is Not Rude. If you love your brother you will honour him, not be rude or offensive; neither will you make jokes at his expense, thus causing him to feel ridiculed. Even teasing can cause hurt and must be avoided. Do not offend a brother or sister simply to get a cheap laugh at his or her expense.

G) It is Not Self-Seeking. In the flesh we want everyone else to be concerned about us. In the Spirit we are concerned about the welfare of others. And we are called to walk in the Spirit, not after the flesh! It is in giving, you will receive!

H) It is Not Easily Angered. It is certain that others will fail at times in their covenant responsibilities towards you. This will be a test of your attitude towards them. It will help you to remember that you have all too often failed others – and the Lord. He has not become angry with you, but has been loving and patient, ready to forgive you for your failures. Do likewise!

I) Keeps No Record of Wrongs. When God forgives, He forgets. He puts your sins behind Him and will never allow them to influence His present or future relationship with you. "I will forgive you, but I will never forget," is not true forgiveness. It requires much grace to treat someone as if he or she had never wronged you, hurt you, failed you or spoken against you. Nevertheless God is able to give you such grace because this is His will for you.

J) Does Not Delight in Evil. If your brother or sister in Christ suffers some setback or fails you in some way, you do not rejoice, neither do you want to spread rumours of his downfall. Because you belong to him and he to you, if he rejoices, you rejoice; if he suffers, you suffer. If he is sick you are concerned to see him healed. If he falls in some way, you want to see him restored.

K) Rejoices with the Truth. Likewise, you rejoice with your brethren when they do well and are blessed, even if at that same time you are going through a period of great struggle and difficulty. You will often be amazed at how quickly God begins to move to meet your need, either directly or through others, as soon as you rejoice in the good that others experience.

L) Always Protects. You want to protect and defend your brother, not expose them to harm. You will stand with them in prayer and against every device of the devil to sow negativity or unbelief into their hearts and lives. And you will defend him against criticism and judgement from others!

M) Always Trusts. Your love for God enables you to trust Him, and He will never fail you. Your love for others will enable you to trust them, and sometimes they will fail you! That is the difference! You do not have any brothers or sisters that reflect the love of Jesus perfectly. You will learn that some are more trustworthy than others, and that it is wise not to trust those who will certainly betray such trust, for they are not in true covenant relationship either with God or you. Regardless of the performance of others, we should always seek to be trustworthy! We are not to "go it alone"; so we have to join hands with others, trust them, and seek to fulfil God's will for His body together. There is no alternative option!

N) Always Hopes. True love anticipates the best, and does not live in expectation of the negative. So, as covenant brothers and sisters, we stand together in expectation that God will work His purpose out among us as we seek to live in love for one another, and so honour Him! We will not give up on others, just as Jesus never gives up on us!

O) Always Perseveres. Love does not give up on people just as you do not want them to give up on you! It is great that in the Body of Christ, when one is struggling the others around him can encourage him. At other times, he will be able to reciprocate, encouraging those who were encouraging him when he was going through a difficult time. In this way we can encourage on another to persevere in faith and love, and not give up. There is much in Scripture about such perseverance – and the reward it reaps.

P) Love Never Fails. This is certainly true of God's love for us. And it is also true of His love in us, whenever we allow that love to come forth and be expressed to others. It is amazing the fruit that such love can produce! So we can only fail when we fail to express His love! Why not have a positive attitude? By the grace of God, do not expect to fail; believe that His love will flow out of you as a river of the Holy Spirit's life!

AS I HAVE LOVED YOU

What does it mean to live in covenant love, to lay down our lives for our friends?

Basically, it means that you live for others, rather than yourself. You are prepared to die to self in order to give to others, to allow the love and life of God that is within you by the Holy Spirit to flow out of you to others around you. **You are able to be a channel of God's love and grace to others!** When Christians relate together in such love, they find that God's love flows out of them in other situations as well.

> YOU ARE ABLE TO BE A CHANNEL OF GOD'S LOVE AND GRACE TO OTHERS!

Covenant love was even expressed in the Old Testament times, especially in the relationship between David and Jonathan:

> *Jonathan became one in spirit with David, and he loved*
> *him as himself…And Jonathan made a covenant with*
> *David because he loved him as himself.*
> *(1 Samuel 18: 1,3)*

Such a relationship was in stark contrast with the way Jonathan's father, King Saul, regarded David. He was angry and jealous of David and wanted to kill him. Jonathan was even prepared to protect David and take his side against his father, so strong was their bond of covenant love.

THIS IS TRUE LOVE: HONOURING YOUR BROTHER ABOVE YOURSELF.

This is all the more remarkable because in the natural order of things, Jonathan would have become the next king. Instead he honours David, recognising him as the one chosen by God, and he does this without any bitter or jealous feelings towards him. **This is true love: honouring your brother above yourself.**

The covenant between Jonathan and David even extended to His descendants, so great was the love between them. After Jonathan's death, David asks:

> *"Is there anyone still left of the house of Saul to whom I can show kindness for Jonathan's sake?" (2 Samuel 9: 1)*

Only Jonathan's crippled son, Mephibosheth, had survived. David showed him "kindness for the sake of your father Jonathan," by restoring all the land that had belonged to his grandfather, Saul, and by having Mephibosheth always eat at his table – a real sign of covenant.

Whenever you look in the New Testament, in the gospels, the epistles, or in the Acts of the Apostles, you see teaching about the nature of love and its practical outworking among the believers.

There is insufficient space to cover all this teaching. Below are seven principles, which need to be expressed in the covenant relationships between believers. Some like to incorporate such principles in a written form of covenant. It is essential that these principles are deeply grafted into the heart of the every believer, whether he is part of a more formal covenant or not. From the time a person is born again, God places him or her in a covenant relationship first with Himself, and then with other believers in the Body of Christ.

These seven principles need to be expressed in the Christian church everywhere. These are not the only principles of which the scriptures speak, but they are essential if the believers' love for one another is real.

Each one of these principles reflects something of our relationship with God, for we are to relate to one another as we relate to Him. Such love will lead to positive action and the willingness to stand against any negative that would undermine these positive principles in our lives.

1. I BELONG TO YOU AND YOU TO ME.

As those who are part of the New Covenant we belong to God. Paul says we "belong to another, to him who was raised from the dead, in order to bear fruit to God." (Romans 7: 4) We therefore belong also to one another:

> *So in Christ we who are many form one body, and each member belongs to all the others. (Romans 12: 5)*

Such a sense of belonging can never be accomplished by people hopping from one church to another. Often this is a device to prevent Christians from facing their covenant responsibilities to one another. Just as you cannot jump from one family to another, so you cannot meaningfully go from one congregation to another. You have to belong to a specific group of people with whom you can outwork the principles of covenant, even when things seem difficult!

Of course there is a sense in which you belong to every other Christian in the world. However, it is impossible to express what the New Testament teaches about covenant love unless you are committed to a specific group of believers.

Jesus related to the crowds wherever He went. He sent out seventy-two disciples on one occasion. He had loving relationships with Mary, Martha, and Lazarus at Bethany, with the women who travelled with the disciples to care for their practical needs. Yet Jesus had twelve disciples as a kind of covenant group. He was involved more deeply with them than with others.

Even within the twelve Jesus had a particularly close relationship with Peter, James, and John. And John is described as "the disciple whom Jesus loved." So Jesus had a variety of relationships, as we all have. To have a true sense of belonging to one another we need to spend time together, more than an hour or two a week at a church service. In the early church, they devoted themselves to fellowship, to the sharing of their lives:

Every day they continued to meet together in the temple courts.
They broke bread in their homes and ate together with glad
and sincere hearts. (Acts 2: 46)

What was the fruit of such love for one another?

"The Lord added to their number daily those
who were being saved." (Acts 2:47)

Already the prayer of Jesus is being answered, that those who become believers would be one, so that the world would believe; that they would love one another in such a way that others would know that Jesus is God's Son, and would be saved!

Why do we not see such effective evangelism in many churches today? Because we do not see such love in many churches today!

By the time of this description of the early church, thousands had become believers in Jerusalem alone. This was the life-style into which they were introduced. This is the lifestyle in a few churches today, and when this is the case, you see the same fruit today: the Lord adding to their number daily those who are being saved.

You may want to protest that it is not possible to come together every day, as those hundreds of early believers were in the habit of doing. The truth is that we adopt the life-style we consider important! It may not be practical for all believers to live in such a way; but they could certainly spend more time together if they so desired, and if there was a true sense of covenant responsibility for one another, as encouraged in scripture.

In Acts we read that *"all the believers were one in heart and mind." (Acts 4: 32)* We see also that *"there was no needy persons among them," (verse 34)* such as was their love for one another expressed in their caring for one another in practical ways.

2. I LOVE YOU AND AM WILLING FOR YOU TO LOVE ME.

This sense of belonging is expressed in the ways in which we give and receive love within the Christian fellowship. Again, this is a reflection of the way in which God loves us:

> *How great is the love the Father has lavished on us, that we should be called children of God! And that is what we are! (1 John 3: 1)*

The Lord desires to see that love *"made complete"* by the way in which we express that love to one another.

> *And so we know and rely on the love God has for us.*
> *God is love. Whoever lives in love lives in God, and God in him.*
> *In this way, love is made complete among us so that we will have*
> *confidence on the day of judgement, because in this world*
> *we are like him. (1 John 4: 16-17)*

THE MORE WE LOVE, THE MORE LIKE JESUS WE BECOME, FOR HE IS LOVE.

This is God's purpose that we should be His witnesses in the world. He has given us His Spirit to enable this. The more we love one another, the more effective our witness. Such obedience to the outworking of His will give us confidence on the day of judgement. **The more we love, the more like Jesus we become, for He is love.**

Such love is expressed in giving. God expressed His love for a sinful world in giving His Son, His very best, to be the Saviour and great High Priest of our salvation. Now He gives His Body of believers as a witness of that love. For wherever there is such love for one another, not only will people be drawn into the Kingdom of God, His people will also reach out with the love, compassion, mercy and grace of God to touch the lives of the lost, the poor, the desperate and needy - as Jesus did!

However, if we love one another as Jesus has loved us, we must not only be prepared to give to others, to bless, serve, encourage and provide for them; we must also be prepared to receive from our brothers and sisters in Christ. Love in the Body of Christ has to be mutual: giving and receiving. You prevent your covenant brother or sister from loving you, if you do not allow him or her to give to you, to bless you, encourage you or help meet your need if it is in his or her power to do so.

Pride, self- sufficiency, and independence are therefore great enemies of covenant love! We are to walk humbly before one another and not be afraid to share need with one another.

This is not a recipe for manipulation, which is an absence of true love; neither is it an encouragement to lazy 'spongers'! The Word of God speaks of giving and receiving, sowing and reaping, blessing and being blessed.

PRIDE, SELF- SUFFICIENCY, AND INDEPENDENCE ARE THEREFORE GREAT ENEMIES OF COVENANT LOVE!

Jesus teaches us the principle that we reap what we sow. To sow love is to reap love. To sow blessing will lead to reaping blessing. Those who encourage will themselves be encouraged. And those who meet the needs of others will themselves have every need met.

3. I WILL PROVIDE FOR YOU WHEN I AM ABLE AND WILL NOT WITHHOLD WHAT I CAN DO TO BLESS YOU.

The meeting of need is one of the practical outworking of our love for one another. We love with actions, not with words. The welfare state is no substitute for such love among believers!

> *If anyone has material possessions and sees his brother in need but has no pity on him, how can the love of God be in him? (1 John 3: 17)*

The way the first Christians even sold property to enable them to meet the needs of fellow believers is held up to us as an example in scripture.

> *For from time to time those who owned times lands or houses old them, brought the money from the sales and put it at the apostles' feet, and it was distributed to anyone as he had need. (Acts 4: 34)*

We can thank God when such love is evidenced today – and it is! The principle by which **all** the believers lived was that *"no one claimed that any of his possessions was his own, but they shared everything they had." (Acts 4: 32)* Having lived by this principle for much of my life I know from personal experience what a liberating way of life it is. Do you own your possessions or do they own you?

However, the important principle is this: we count people as more important than our possessions! We would all agree to this in theory; but what of the practical outworking?

Jesus taught us that whatever we do to the least of His brothers we do to Him. And this is how we need to understand covenant love. Whenever I give to my brother or sister in Christ, I am giving to Him. Whatever I do to them, I do to Him. If I withhold what I could give, I withhold from Him!

This is not inviting foolishness in the use of our money or property, for Paul warns us that even if we give away all that we have, but without love, we gain nothing. God will only measure back the increase when we give in love.

Ananaias and Sapphira gave with deceitful hearts not with love, and were judged accordingly! No wonder great awe was upon the people, for they understood that God not only sees what we give, but the motive that lies behind the giving.

We are, then, to give in love for our brothers and sisters, because we care for them, not because we have a legalistic obligation towards them.

4. I WILL DEFEND YOU AGAINST ANY WHO SPEAK OR ACT AGAINST YOU, AND WILL REFUSE TO SPEAK NEGATIVELY OF YOU MYSELF.

This is another very important aspect of covenant love, for you cannot love someone while also speaking ill of them, or listen to others running them down by the things they say about them. Love is kind, not vindictive.

Gossip is always to be avoided. You do not want others to talk about you behind your back; so do not talk about them in such a way!

When others are critical of someone, your silence is usually taken as agreement. The critics will even tell others that you agreed with them – because you do not disagree! So it is important to refuse to listen to negative criticism and gossip, and make it clear that you do not agree with any verbal attacks as your brothers and sisters in Christ.

There will be some matters about which you will disagree with others. Christians should also be able to handle disagreement in love, without being critical of the one with whom you disagree!

5. I WILL HONOUR YOU AND WILL OBEY THOSE WHO ARE OVER ME IN THE LORD.

When you consider the nature of God's love that is to be reflected in us, it is clear that you cannot love your brother or sister without treating him or her with the respect and honour expected by the Lord. You show respect for people by the right attitude you maintain towards them. You honour them by giving to them, serving them in any way you can as a sign of that respect.

You are to give double honour, God says, to those who are over you in the Lord. They are responsible to the Lord not only for themselves, but also for those they lead. Not to honour them is to make their life more difficult. To honour them is a reflection of your submission to the authority of God Himself. It is He who has placed you under them, for your good – to lead you, disciple you, train and equip you for ministry.

It is clear from Scripture that God regards disobedience to those He places in authority as rebellion against Him, and this has serious consequences. Of course this shows how important it is to ensure that you are under true spiritual authority and are not subject to someone who has raised himself up, and seeks to control others to maintain his position.

6. I WILL BE FAITHFUL TO YOU AND WILL NOT TREAT MY COVENANT RESPONSIBILITIES LIGHTLY

In Scripture, faithfulness is a key word in the understanding and outworking of covenant. God has always been faithful to His covenant promises, even when Israel persistently disobeyed and failed to keep covenant with Him. It is inconceivable that He would ever fail to fulfil a promise He has given.

He wants to see such consistency expressed in our relationships with one another. These are not to be based on emotion, neither are they dependant on the performance of those we are called to love.

Feelings have little to do with covenant love. Your responsibility is to bless, give, serve, encourage and be faithful, regardless of your personal failings and circumstances. Neither is your love to be affected by the ways others respond, or fail to respond, to that love. The Lord wants you to show a consistency in your devotion to others, no matter how they treat you. As you grow in the outworking of covenant love, you are able to do this more readily.

Nobody pretends this is easy. We need to follow Jesus, who showed consistency by loving even His enemies and those who hated Him. As far as His loved ones are concerned, He never judged or condemned them, even when they failed. He forgave the disciples when they deserted Him at His hour of greatest need, and restored Peter when he denied Him three times!

7. I WILL FORGIVE YOU. I WILL NOT ALLOW ANY FAILURE ON YOUR PART TO HINDER OUR RELATIONSHIP. IF I FAIL IN MY LOVE FOR YOU, I SHALL BE QUICK TO ASK FOR YOUR FORGIVENESS.

Being human, we are fallible and we shall inevitably fail at times. This does not mean that we expect to fail, but that we need to know how to cope with failure, both that of others and our own.

Jesus' remedy is very simple – *FORGIVE*. No matter how often your brother sins against you, forgive him. Seven times in a single day! Seventy times seven, infinitely! This is the way God has to forgive you, and how you are to forgive others.

Divisions among Christians are not so much caused by wrong treatment of each other (that will inevitably happen at times), but in failing to react in a right and godly way to such treatment. People leave churches with an attitude of offense which is a grave sin on their part, for it is clear they have not forgiven those who caused the offense.

It is not a matter of who is right or wrong, but fulfilling our covenant responsibility to pray and work through any difficulties that arise. Remember that Jesus warned that if we fail to forgive those who sin against us, God will not forgive us! This means that the person who holds onto offense is in real trouble, not only with others but with God Himself.

People who carry offense take that offense with them wherever they go. It spreads from them to others like a negative spiritual cancer. Usually it is not long before they take offense again, and leave yet another church! This is the very opposite of covenant love!

Forgiveness can prevent a situation from becoming worse and can keep relationships sweet. We learn to have forgiving hearts, reacting with forgiveness instead of offense.

Those who have set their hearts on covenant, on obeying Jesus, will not *deliberately* sin against their brethren. But there may be occasions when they inadvertently or unintentionally grieve and fail others. It is always right to be quick to confess your sin, or any wrong reaction to the sins of others. Often you will need to do this face to face with those involved. All this is part of our covenant love for our brothers and sisters in Christ.

EYES ON JESUS

The writer to Hebrews tells us to fix our eyes on Jesus and consider Him. This is essential in the outworking of covenant in our lives. You will find it difficult to cope with what others do to you at times! It is easy to be judgemental and critical of them, quick to see their failures and slow to face your own. **Keeping your eyes on Jesus will help you to remain merciful.**

Unless you want to glorify Jesus, you can become proud, imagining that you are better at covenant relationships than others, losing sight of the fact that apart from Him you can do nothing. **You can only hope to live a life of covenant love by trusting in His grace!**

Faith working through love! Paul says this is the only thing that counts. For without faith we cannot please God, and without love we cannot obey Him.

It seems we began on such a positive note about covenant and end on several negative notes. We have to face honestly and realistically what it means to live in covenant love. However, remember what Jesus said when commanding the disciples to adopt this life-style:

*I have told you this that my joy may be in you and
that your joy may be complete. (John 15: 11)*

**This is a life-style, not an activity; a life-style that gives deep
and lasting joy, the joy of knowing you are fulfilling the
purpose to which God has called you.**

You are united with Jesus Himself in this joy. Even when others
seem difficult to love, you will be amazed at the way the Holy
Spirit gives you a real heart of love for those people, if you are only
willing to persevere.

Do not be deterred by your failure. Anyone who thinks he or she
is good at loving others lives in self-deception. You will find that
the most loving people never see themselves in that way. They are
too busy dealing with the unloving actions and reactions that still
need to be refined out of their hearts!

As we keep our eyes on Jesus, our great High Priest, we live
continually in the awareness that He represents us before the
Father, He intercedes for us with His blood that cleanses away our
sins and failures.

He serves us from heaven in the power of His indestructible and
endless life, pouring into our hearts the love that we need.
Remember why He has initiated the new covenant, and why it
contains this vital new commandment: **that the world may
believe!**

Jesus knows that to see the Church's great commission fulfilled we will need to love one another, for He said that we are to go into all the world to make *disciples* of all nations, baptising them –

> *And teaching them to obey everything*
> *I have commanded you. And surely I am with you always,*
> *to the very end of the age. (Matthew 28: 20)*

The True Series will comprise the following titles:

TRUE ANOINTING
TRUE APOSTLES
TRUE AUTHORITY
TRUE CHURCH
TRUE COVENANT
TRUE DELIVERANCE
TRUE DEVOTION
TRUE DISCIPLES
TRUE FAITH
TRUE FREEDOM
TRUE GRACE
TRUE HEALING
TRUE HOLINESS
TRUE JUDGMENT
TRUE KINGDOM
TRUE LIFE
TRUE LORD
TRUE LOVE
TRUE MISSION
TRUE PRAYER
TRUE SALVATION
TRUE WISDOM
TRUE WORSHIP

All these books by Colin Urquhart and a catalogue of other titles and teaching materials can be obtained from:

Kingdom Faith Resources, Roffey Place, Old Crawley Road
Faygate, Horsham, West Sussex RH12 4RU.
Telephone 01293 854 600 email: resources@kingdomfaith.com